TITANIC'S
TRAGIC JOURNEY

A FLY on the WALL
HISTORY

BY THOMAS KINGSLEY TROUPE   ILLUSTRATED BY JOMIKE TEJIDO

PICTURE WINDOW BOOKS
a capstone imprint

Hi, I'm Maggie, and this is my brother, Horace.

We've been "flies on the wall" during important events in history.

We saw Albert Einstein make some amazing scientific discoveries.

$$E = mc^2$$

We rode along on Paul Revere's midnight ride.

We even cheered for boxer Cassius Clay (later known as Muhammad Ali) when he won an Olympic gold medal!

One bit of history we'll never forget? The one and only voyage of a very famous ship . . . .

Horace and I were flying around Southampton, England, in April 1912. There were a lot of people crowded near the water. Some of them carried suitcases. Others walked up a ramp toward a huge ship called RMS *Titanic*.

I don't like boats or ships. I get seasick, and it's not pretty. The people gathered around the ship were excited, though. I heard someone call it "unsinkable." So Horace and I decided to take a closer look.

* * *

About 2,232 people boarded *Titanic*: 1,324 passengers and 908 crew members.

* * *

What's going on here, Maggie?

It sounds like *Titanic* is sailing to the United States.

Many of these people are going there to start new lives.

Titanic was huge. It measured nearly three football fields in length! It had restaurants, libraries, and barbershops. It even had a gym and a swimming pool.

The ship was about to set sail on its "maiden voyage." That meant it was going on a trip for the very first time. I wanted to buzz off *Titanic*. But Horace wanted to stay, so we did.

HONNNNNK! A giant horn let everyone know the ship was leaving the dock. The sound nearly knocked off my wings!

✦ ✦ ✦

Titanic almost had an accident as it left the Southampton port. A steamship named *New York* nearly crashed into its side.

✦ ✦ ✦

4

Those little boats
are dragging Titanic
out of the harbor.

Can't it move
on its own?

I would think so.

But maybe big
ships can't start
their engines this
close to land.

Passengers waved to the people who watched *Titanic* sail away. Some of the people left behind looked sad. Horace guessed they were already missing their loved ones.

I always feel less seasick indoors, so we flew into a room on the upper deck. Inside was a man in a uniform named Captain Edward J. Smith. He was in charge of *Titanic* and getting everyone to New York City safely.

Wow! See that big wheel back there, Horace?

Is that how Captain Smith steers the ship?

Maybe.

I think the levers next to it send messages to the rest of the crew.

So, which one sends a sandwich up here?

* * *

White Star Lines was the company that built *Titanic*. The head of White Star Lines personally picked Captain Smith to command the ship.

* * *

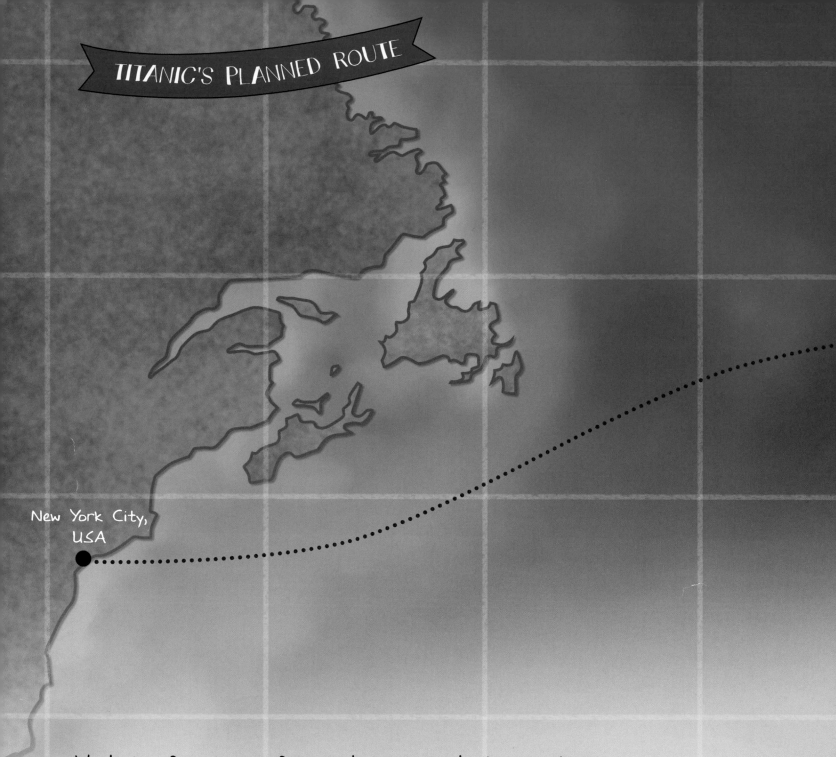

TITANIC'S PLANNED ROUTE

New York City,
USA

We had a few stops before we headed to the United States.
The ship stopped in Cherbourg, France, and then Queenstown, Ireland.
A few people got off, but even more people got on.

After our stop in Ireland, *Titanic* headed for the open seas. I didn't
know if I was really ready for the trip. But it was too late to turn
back. The land grew smaller and smaller behind us. Next stop, New York!

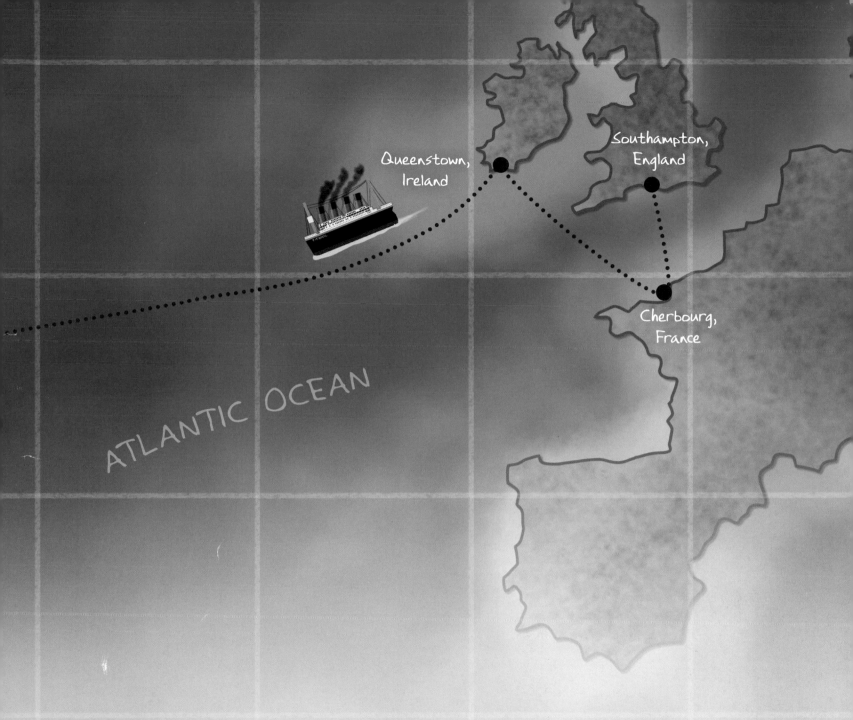

ATLANTIC OCEAN

Queenstown, Ireland

Southampton, England

Cherbourg, France

Maggie, it looks like *TITANIC* is sailing across the ATLANTIC.

Hey, that kind of rhymes! I never knew I was a poet . . .

We're going to be on this ship for about a week?

Oof! Suddenly I don't feel so good.

* * *

Titanic's top speed was 23 knots. That's the same as 26 miles (37 kilometers) per hour.

* * *

Since we had a long trip ahead, Horace and I decided to explore every inch of the ship. We left the upper deck and soon found the first-class reception room. Well-dressed people were eating some delicious-looking food. Waiters brought the diners whatever they wanted to eat or drink.

A group of men played music. People talked and laughed. I had never seen such a lavish ship before. Even the staircase going up to the guest rooms looked expensive.

Wow. Look at the tasty treats, Maggie!

They don't smell as good as the garbage I ate this morning, but . . .

Horace!

Don't fly so close!

The diners don't want flies in their frosting!

* * *

Titanic's orchestra was made up of eight musicians. Everyone in the band knew how to play 352 songs.

* * *

Horace and I flew upstairs to see more of the ship. We followed a man into his first-class suite. I wasn't sure what a suite was, but Horace and I both love sweets, so . . .

* * *

In 1912, a first-class ticket on *Titanic* cost between about $146 and $4,250.
A second-class ticket was about $60, and a third-class ticket was between about $15 and $40.

* * *

I found out that a suite is where some of the first-class people stayed. Each suite had two bedrooms, a sitting room, and a bathroom. It even had a private balcony from which to view the ocean.

This man said he was going to meet someone for a game of squash.

Squash? Ooh, as a fly, I really don't like the sound of that!

I think you're supposed to squash a ball, not the other player, Horace.

Since the squash players didn't want us around, Horace and I went
deeper into the ship. We found the third-class passengers down there.
Their rooms were very plain — nothing like first class.

We flew even further belowdecks, until we got to a large, super-hot room. Men were working hard. They shoveled coal into furnaces nonstop. Horace heard them call it a boiler room. They weren't kidding. It was boiling!

Why are those guys shoveling all that coal?

Are they trying to get dirty?

Coal is the fuel *Titanic* needs to keep its engines going.

It's like gasoline for a car.

A ship this big needs a lot of fuel.

* * *

More than 600 tons (544 metric tons) of coal per day were needed to keep *Titanic* running.

* * *

(about 9:30 p.m.)

We stayed out of trouble for the next few days. The ship was running fine, and people were enjoying the trip to New York. There were lots of new rooms to explore. I wasn't sure we'd ever see them all.

Horace wanted to check out a small room on the upper deck. It was called the Marconi room. Inside were radios and lots of wires. Two men were sending and receiving messages through the machines. A few of the incoming messages got me worried. They warned about icebergs in Titanic's path.

Uh-oh, Horace. Look at this.

It's another iceberg warning from a nearby ship.

But these guys are too busy sending out messages from the passengers to notice.

They need to pay attention!

* * *

The first warning about icebergs in the Atlantic Ocean reached *Titanic* on April 14 around 9 a.m. The ship may have received as many as six warnings throughout the day. It's believed that only two reached Captain Smith.

* * *

Horace and I wanted to look for ourselves,
so we flew up to the crow's nest. Horace doesn't like heights,
but we flew up there anyway. We joined two men on lookout
duty. The night was so dark! It was tough to see anything.

Then, around 11:30 p.m., one of the lookouts rang the bell three times.
He picked up the phone and shouted, "Iceberg right ahead!"

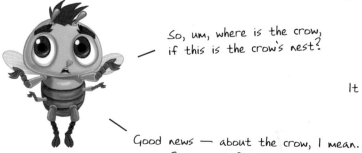

So, um, where is the crow,
if this is the crow's nest?

Good news — about the crow, I mean.
Crows eat flies, you know.

But bad news about the iceberg!

It isn't an actual crow's nest, Horace.

Besides, *Titanic* has much bigger
problems right now!

The iceberg was coming up fast. We wanted to see if *Titanic* was going to hit it. Horace and I flew down to the bow as fast as we could. We heard a loud groaning sound along the right side of the ship.

The officers shouted to one another, "Turn the ship! Turn the ship!" They weren't able to steer it quickly enough, though. Chunks of ice broke off the iceberg and landed on the deck. Surprisingly, most of the passengers didn't even notice.

The iceberg was said to have been 50 to 100 feet (15-30 meters) high and 200 to 400 feet (61-122 m) long.
For comparison, a football field is 300 feet (91 m) long.

About an hour later, a crew member reported that *Titanic* was leaking. Horace and I buzzed belowdecks to see. Water poured into the hallways. People ran, splashing through the water, trying to get to the upper decks.

It didn't make sense! They had steered *Titanic* away from the iceberg, and it looked like we'd missed a direct hit. But the ship filled with water. The engines stopped. *Titanic*, the "unsinkable" ship, was in danger of sinking.

What is everyone going to do, Maggie?

This is really bad!

I know!

Hopefully they'll be able to call for help and get everyone into the lifeboats!

* * *

The iceberg sliced into *Titanic*'s hull in six places. Each slit was no wider than a human hand.

* * *

People were scared. Crew members raced to help women and children into the lifeboats. Horace counted and saw that there wasn't going to be enough room on the boats for everyone. Some lifeboats were lowered to the water before they were even half full.

The men in the Marconi room radioed for help. Someone shot a flare into the night sky. Its bright light was supposed to lead other ships to *Titanic*. Time was running out!

Titanic carried 20 lifeboats. Laws back then said ships didn't need to carry any more, although the boats had room for only one-third of the total number of passengers and crew.

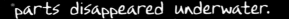

* * *

It took nearly three hours for *Titanic* to completely sink into the Atlantic Ocean.

* * *

On April 15, 1915, around 4 a.m., the survivors of *Titanic* saw hope. A ship called the RMS *Carpathia* arrived. The captain dodged six icebergs on the way to the rescue. His men lowered boats and helped the survivors onto *Carpathia*. Four hours later, the ship set sail for New York.

A total of 705 people survived the *Titanic* disaster. More than 1,500 people died. *Titanic's* sinking led to the start of the International Ice Patrol. Part of the U.S. Coast Guard, the Ice Patrol warns ships about dangerous icebergs in their path.

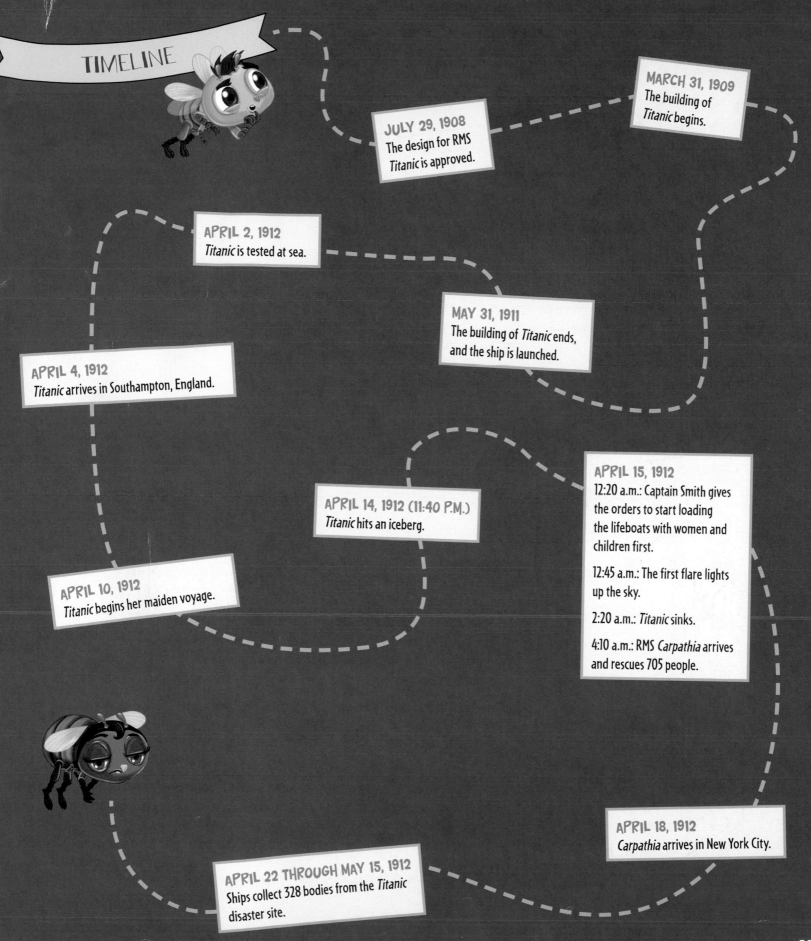

TIMELINE

JULY 29, 1908
The design for RMS *Titanic* is approved.

MARCH 31, 1909
The building of *Titanic* begins.

APRIL 2, 1912
Titanic is tested at sea.

MAY 31, 1911
The building of *Titanic* ends, and the ship is launched.

APRIL 4, 1912
Titanic arrives in Southampton, England.

APRIL 14, 1912 (11:40 P.M.)
Titanic hits an iceberg.

APRIL 15, 1912
12:20 a.m.: Captain Smith gives the orders to start loading the lifeboats with women and children first.

12:45 a.m.: The first flare lights up the sky.

2:20 a.m.: *Titanic* sinks.

4:10 a.m.: RMS *Carpathia* arrives and rescues 705 people.

APRIL 10, 1912
Titanic begins her maiden voyage.

APRIL 18, 1912
Carpathia arrives in New York City.

APRIL 22 THROUGH MAY 15, 1912
Ships collect 328 bodies from the *Titanic* disaster site.

GLOSSARY

bow–the front end of a ship

crow's nest–a lookout post located high above a ship

deck–a floor on a ship

furnace–a large, enclosed metal chamber in which fuel is burned to produce heat

hull–the main body of a boat

knot–a unit of speed measurement

lavish–very fancy

maiden–the very first

port–a harbor where ships dock safely

reception room–a gathering place where people can talk and eat

RMS–an abbreviation for Royal Mail Ship; RMS ships are registered to carry mail for the United Kingdom postal service

squash–a game played with rackets and a small rubber ball on an enclosed court

suite–a number of connected rooms

tragic–very sad

THINK ABOUT IT

1. Many people called *Titanic* "the unsinkable ship." Why do you think they believed that?

2. Looking at the illustrations on pages 12 through 14, compare and contrast *Titanic's* first-class suites with its third-class rooms.

3. Describe the Marconi room – where it was, what it looked like, what its purpose was, and why it was important to the ship.

READ MORE

Adams, Simon. *DK Eyewitness Books:* Titanic. New York: DK Children, 2014.

Gregory, Josh. *If You Were a Kid Aboard the* Titanic. New York: Scholastic, 2017.

Temple, Bob. *The* Titanic: *An Interactive History Adventure.* Mankato, Minn.: Capstone, 2016.

INTERNET SITES

Use FactHound to find Internet sites related to this book:

Visit *www.facthound.com*

Just type in 9781515815990 and go.

Super-cool stuff!

Check out projects, games and lots more at
www.capstonekids.com

INDEX

Look for other books in the series:

Special thanks to our adviser, Kevin Byrne, PhD, Professor Emeritus of History, Gustavus Adolphus College, for his expertise.

Picture Window Books is published by Capstone,
1710 Roe Crest Drive, North Mankato, Minnesota 56003
www.mycapstone.com

Library of Congress Cataloging-in-Publication data is available on the Library of Congress website.
ISBN 978-1-5158-1599-0 (library binding)
ISBN 978-1-5158-1603-4 (paperback)
ISBN 978-1-5158-1607-2 (eBook PDF)

Summary: Describes the events leading up to and including the sinking of *Titanic* in the Atlantic Ocean on April 15, 1912.

Editor: Jill Kalz
Designer: Sarah Bennett
Creative Director: Nathan Gassman
Production Specialist: Laura Manthe

The illustrations in this book were planned with pencil on paper and finished with digital paints.

Printed and bound in the United States of America.
010850S18